Sailing To the Edges

poems by

Jennifer M Phillips

Finishing Line Press
Georgetown, Kentucky

Sailing To the Edges

ACKNOWLEDGMENTS

"The Icon of Extreme Humility" was a finalist, in *Cutthroat Magazine*'s Joy
Harjo Poetry Prize 2023, and published in *Cutthroat's Prize Anthology*, 2024.

Publisher: Leah Huete de Maines
Editor: Christen Kincaid
Cover Art: Jennifer M Phillips
Author Photo: Jennifer M Phillips
Cover Design: Elizabeth Maines McCleavy

Order online: www.finishinglinepress.com
also available on amazon.com

Author inquiries and mail orders:
Finishing Line Press
PO Box 1626
Georgetown, Kentucky 40324
USA

Contents

Part 1. On the Belgica

Sailing With Roald Amundsen on the Belgica To Antarctica, 1897-1899

Put me on skis and I can overpass mountains, rails
deep in spindrift powder, scour my teeth with ice.
Ply me with Akavit by the fire: I dream of poles
and expeditions, I hire or breed sled dogs, slice
cord for tent tie-downs, crease canvas into bales
for packing. Photographed: my face is wind-chiseled basalt
rising from a surf of Inuit-chewed seal-hide.
By twenty-five, fur-britched like a bear, as First Mate
on the Belgica, I hit my stride
beside Captain Adrien de Gerlache de Gomery.
We set sail for Antarctica in 1897.
Heaven for this Viking-scion—South by sea
to earth's end, hell on earth—but my heaven
in wind, in men, in snow, in ocean.

(16th August 1897)

Cannon-fire out of Antwerp, crowds cheering,
benefactors' tossed hats as our Belgica slipped her mooring,
nineteen of us young men in our high hopes waving.
What a ship! 150 horses of steam straining
to gallop, a great mane of sail above. 35 meters long
and three masts, reinforced, a buttressed hull strong
against ice, felt-lined for warmth, laboratory
equipped for investigation, archives and library.
Born the sea-yacht *Patria* in Sandefjord
every inch was refurbished, strut and board
spit-shone and hope-filled for the venture
for science and boundary-breaking, pure
joy and a measure of tingling terror
whip-stinging us forward into our vocation's measure.

The first night out, the steam boiler quit,
along with three sailors. They say it's bad luck to rename a ship!
And shameful somehow to limp into Ostend
by sail, like a marathoner who at the first bend
must pull up to tip a stone out of his shoe
under public gaze. Just a day or two
and we were underway to Cape Adare
where four would land for research, while from there
we'd sail on to Melbourne and chart Pacific isles,
observing people, plants, birds, whales, and seals;
plumbing depths, and taking measures of location,
height and size of lands, making notation
for new maps. Our doctor and master of navigation:
Frederick Cook, my old rival in polar exploration.

Two months later, the equator crossed.
First-timers were fat-and-soot-soaped, then shaved
bare with a wooden razor, and bucket-baptized
by King Neptune (our Captain), then we all feasted.
Like a bad ballad, our drunk chef got into a fight
and navvies from Chile had to be fetched on board
to haul him off. Some sailors were chronically tight
and peevish, some were green, some grew bored
with the project. The meals dished out by the new cook
were burnt and inadequate, enough to make you sick
if the heaving sea didn't. Tierra del Fuego rounded
in early December, we needed provisions and landed
among friendly people. We started a glossary
of their language. Then, hove back to the sea.

New Year's night, we ran aground on a great rock!
The old chart failed us. There was a mighty crack
and we stuck fast there. Had to out-wait the tide
for a lift, but no luck. Tons of coal were heaved over the side,
and some of our precious fresh water. Twenty-two hours—we feared
we would split on the ledge where we groaned, and stayed speared.
A new tide rose. Engine wound full, all sail raised,
a wonder! We broke free, largely whole. Then we repaired
the stove-in wood with timber the Fuegans gave us.
That language of theirs we learned had helped to save us.
We left friends there, and that little crowd waving us out
felt gladder than Antwerp's grand farewell from home port.
Down Drake's Passage we took soundings all the way.
Below us, two thousand fathoms of green sway.

The sea was a pecked iron platter under overcast,
as we bumped our first small iceberg in blinding snow.
The lookout could barely see past the mast,
to find the ice-islands buffeting below,
and the waves perturbing our ship were towering higher
than any of us had ever seen before.
We reduced and reefed some sail, straining in terror.
The scuppers clogged with ice. At half-past four,
Seamen Wiencke took an axe and went to clear them
but a great wave rose and swept him overboard.
Our Second, Georges Lecointe rushed out to grab him
but could not hold his grip. The man went down.
Sheer grace, we saved Lecointe from being drowned.

It was a somber sail down that new passage
we added to our maps. We counted more
than seventy islands. Lecointe had skill to gauge
by eye their dimensions. Good work, but hearts sore
with loss, we named one after Weincke,
having no body for our prayers to commend
in a quiet cove where we paused and set our anchor.
The Lord who stilled the waters with a word
will surely find and raise him at the last,
good lad, alongside us, to his reward.
On the Antarctic peninsula, our botanist
added *Deschampsia antarctica* to his new plant horde.
We spotted a flightless fly—that was a first—
Belgica antarctica, wonders—but at such cost!

15th of February, we crossed the circle:
66 degrees and 30 feet South.
Our comrade Emil Racovita was practiced and able
to identify whales and seals, penguins, all the birds:
pipits and fulmars, skuas, godwits and sheath-
bills, petrels and gulls. Daily we heard
their shrill cries from Mt. William's rocky ledges
around the shores of Bellingshausen Sea.
Our microscope was kept busy. Our lengthy sheaf
of observations grew to volumes as we
roamed the shores and ventured inland with our sledges.
Work gave pleasure day after long-lit day.
We gave little thought then to the coming dark
of polar winter, still a season away.

March arrived like a lion, and the temperature
dropped like a plumbline. Abruptly, decks froze
and the ice closed us in before we realized.
So we rolled and packed up our sails, and made sure
the propeller was pulled. We banked down the engine fire
making ready for a long winter in that place.
Sea was more than a kilometer away, far
across the thickening crust of white pack ice.
Great bergs stuck up like monstrous broken teeth,
men tiny as mice beside them. Photographs
Cook took will show us dwarfed and huddled beneath,
as though caught in the mythic jaws of a mammoth.
We heaped up snow house-high around the hull
to preserve what warmth we could, while the wind was still.

"We are no longer navigators; now
we are prisoners doomed to serve out our sentence."
That's how the Captain put it, and he'd allow
that his choice kept us southward, his inner drive intense
to reach the southernmost terminus
no matter at what peril. We had not clothes
sufficient for all or thick enough to warm us.
By May 16th the sun had ceased to rise
and 63 days of constant darkness gripped
that land. We felt grimly inert, motionless,
though pack ice kept moving under us. Our ship slipped
two thousand kilometers that winter, west
in the fathomless cold, tending the little spark
of our lives like a pan of embers through that dark.

When the wind dropped enough we made short, brisk forays
onto the ice, but the cold was brutal.
We were shut in by gales and snow over tedious days.
Our stories all were told. The meals were awful
as the skilless cook spoiled our rations and often burned
up and burned through what little we had.
Spirits plummeted. Men started going mad
with cold and boredom and dread. We all yearned
for light and heat and respite from one another.
June 5—midwinter—Emile Danco's heart
gave out and he died. We had to bury our brother
in an ice-hole we chiseled. Such a bitter hurt
to us all, and our Captain's particular friend.
We pondered in fretful hammocks our own end.

Perhaps when my turn comes, I'll disappear
into a blizzard, or underneath a grey wave.
Truth is, I could never settle for long there
in Norway. My nature's too restless by half!
My legs are too long to take my rest in a bed.
I prefer a snow pillow to soft eider-down.
It takes some pain, and the wrestling in my head,
to feel fully alive and myself and strong—
not to be bested by the worst the wilds can bring
nor my own doubts and devils. I want to learn
something new every day, and work among men
clear and clean as axe-strokes, who also burn
with desire to strike out where no one has yet been
and to cast their eyes on what no one else has seen.

Dr. Cook stepped in to save our hazing minds
with a mandatory Madhouse Promenade
around our ship. He ordered all the hands
to play games, to sing and play the fools to aid
our sanity. He bade us strip to the buff
and stand by a fire, musing ultraviolet light,
though faint, might supply vitamins enough
for our lack of daylight. He'd lived with Inuit
and had us hunt for penguins and seals, and eat
the meat raw, as they did. We all judged it foul,
but some depression lifted. We chewed the fat,
and the exercise of the chase helped some, though not all.
The grinding gears of the weeks wore us down to gloom
as we waned and thinned like ghosts at the Gates of Doom.

A man may see his reflection in the ice
where a surface is scraped clean of snow and detritus:
a face stripped down of excess and adulation,
schooled in solitude, silence, cooperation
among a small band of comrades. They, too,
have left all comfort for the wilds of snow
and the unknown, shirking off society's limits
after more space and knowledge. Polar summits
become a vocation. The whisper of the divine
wakes these men; the devils within
do battle. A man is whittled as by fire
to essentials or to ash. We will not retire
home the same men we were. Married to the quest,
may we never be courted by too easy a rest!

Yet in the depth of winter, stooping to the glass
to find only a haggard, bearded stranger,
most of us fall sullen, chuck a curse
or two at an unoffending brother.
There are weeks we are shut in under these rough boards
as in a coffin walled in a common grave,
while the wind trumpets and wails triumph or grief
over us. Food is short, one of us hoards
bread and is threatened by the rest; yet which
of us has not thought of it? Minds wobble and twitch
as the hull creaks around us in the well of night
where we are sunk, yet surviving. God help the sailor
who sees his beloved dead mirrored over his shoulder,
as omen of his own dwindling from the light!

Two men edged into catatonic despair
by July, when the sun began its slow return
with twenty minutes of daylight—an uncanny glare
after so long subterranean. We hoped to warm
soon. Cook wrote, "We felt buoyant relief,
and new hope surged, hot with life through our arteries."
Three of us took a sledge out onto the shelf
for a six-day trip, hoping we might see
a channel opening through the ice as it thinned.
We were nearly cut off by a crack, but got across
and back to the Belgica. Weeks passed. The sun
glare on snow blinded more than a few of us—fresh
torment, in endless day, but grinding cold,
and the ice did not budge or ever seem to diminish.

Come that September, we were still marooned.
The cold increased—minus 43 centigrade,
the ice thicker than before. We feared we were doomed
to another winter. Men raged and cried
and cursed one another and our whole enterprise.
Mid-October tricked us into a cruel hope
as the ice woke us with cracking and creaking noise—
but still it did not release us from its grip.
In our hold, from Antwerp, we had safe-secured
a hundred-sixty sticks of tonite—like TNT—
so that in a pinch we might blast ourselves free.
We set it with care, lining an escape road,
picturing an explosive blast of release,
and two of us stepped back to light the fuse.

What a roar of thunder all that tonite made,
and snow flew up like a heavenward avalanche
when the fuses blew. But the ice below was hard
as steel and we scored not even a shallow trench
let alone a passage out. We faced the worst:
another season immured. Christmas passed
without celebration. Cook kept us at work
with our research, grim routine in the growing dark.
Poor Adam Tollefsen went steadily insane.
We tended him as we could—it didn't help.
A few had hallucinations. Horrid dreams
or sleeplessness plagued many, as we leaked hope
like a heap of soldiers' shell-punctured canteens.
I kept fear to myself and saved my tears for my dreams.

First, January. Dr. Cook has had a brainwave:
We might chop two shallow channels to the sea
and let open water flow in where we have carved
and it might melt enough ice down to break us free.
A kilometer, with axes and saws and picks,
we dug, before daylight began to dwindle,
and indeed water came in, thinning the thick
ice crust and splitting open a slim channel.
Then a rumble began. The entire sheet started to shift.
In a minute our alley had closed up tight as before.
A month of labor vanished into that rift.
Our only motion, the pack's imperceptible drift.
What a cruel joke of harsh nature to re-inter
our last try for resurrection, and crush us with winter!

Twelfth, February, A literal bolt from the blue:
the ice sheet split, a generous channel gaped wide
from our prow to the ocean. We leapt to build a new
fire in the boiler and unstow and spread the yards
with sail, and set that tough hull forward to chew
through the ice-slushed path now open. It took weeks
of pressing and dodging icebergs to bring us through
to full open water. Amazing—we sprang no leaks,
though our coal was quickly exhausted. So by sail
we made slow passage back to Punta Arenas.
Making port, we kissed the bare ground underneath us,
restocked our provisions, and happily sent mail
home, announcing our planned return.
Our nearly snuffed hearts dared again to burn.

New men with new shaves and newly-minted clothes,
we paraded like lords in front of one another.
We'd looked like cave-creatures or sorry scarecrows,
wan and skinny, half-dead from extremes of weather,
though I think they were glad to see us half-alive,
and we were wined and dined, and slept in beds.
Now, I can confess my own hour of darkest dread,
—perhaps for some others, too—none of us brave
enough to own our grief when our ship's little cat,
Nantsen, died of the dark and the cold last June
and our touch of simple comfort guttered out
like a tiny candle-flame. We each mourned alone.

Fifth November, our remnant sailed into home port.
Three scientists stayed in Chile at their work
in that safer circumstance—such was their heart
for learning! Lifetimes now to report their research.
A band struck up La Barbançonne, the cannons roared
Dignitaries waved from the River Scheldt's shore.
We were fêted and feasted. Lecointe and Captain Gerlache
were hung with gold medals. The King knighted our whole batch
to the Order of Leopold, as *bold servants of civilization*,
or some such palavar, with grandiose state celebration.
That night, alone, curled up next to my fire
with charts, and a cat at my elbow to conspire,
and a snifter of Akavit, I planned again to set sail
with new-sanded skis on a route to the *North* Pole!

*

Part 2: Refit and Relaunch, 2023

52 Degrees Fahrenheit, 78 Degrees Latitude

52 degrees Fahrenheit. I gazed across the placid fjord
to the bowl and swoop and fan-scrape of a beach
where a glacier came and went in the infancy of this far place.

There's little in the way of sidewalks for the tottering.
Bear warning signs stuck at the outskirts of town.
Come young. Learn to shoot a rifle. Befriend the dark.

Only one mine of seven still moles the mountain
They set dockside heaps of export coal in a grid.
More than fifteen feet high, piles may self-ignite.

All dread fire in a wooden town that has burned before.
That killing heat in the winter, everyone fears.
But, I wonder, do the rest of us fear heat enough?

I'm too hot for the parka I have brought
to Svalbard, or even for gloves or a light fleece.
Dovekies come fluttering and flipping between town roofs

in their own black jackets and tiny caps of down.
There's never been so warm a summer here, or anywhere!
The bay wears khaki, churned by tankers and liners

swinging in and out of dock at Longyearbyen.
Explorer tours in flotillas of inflatables
are tooling back and forth between there and here,

measuring whatever it is they seek to measure,
observing what they come here to observe,
sweating in their matching scarlet storm gear.

Could an underwater curtain contain enough cold
to keep a melting glacier from calving away?
Could a sunshade in space chill us enough to survive?

We are watching from altitude on our cruise ship's veranda.
Feathers float on the gloss below. Tundra-skirted hills look
   impassively down.
The wheeling dovekies and terns are watching us.

*

What Latitude?

"If every human lined up facing north with their arms outstretched and touching, at what latitude would this closed circle be?"
—Robert Fizek, Newton, MA 8-12-23 letter to New Scientist, p.46

The children would have to reach up to be included.
Mothers, with babes in arms, might stretch out just one hand,
tentatively
in case of a sudden wriggle.
How could you calculate?
Twelve-year-olds would have disappeared
somewhere with their friends
and the four-year-olds would never stand still long enough to count.
It wouldn't be anywhere too cold, I suppose.
Equatorial? Would we count slant mountains.
Would there be a chain of barges,
and what of storms in mid-ocean?
Horse latitude, maybe, where they threw those creatures
overboard trying to survive their ships' becalming?
Or the doldrums,
where we become too bored to pay attention to the project
and are lost into our scrolling?
We might hope for a vaccine requirement and sanitizer first,
and that the ones next to us
could be people that we know
or might meet in our own neighborhood,
clean-handed ones, we think, like us.
Would we feel the sweat
of those just in from their outdoor labor,
their calluses and blisters
coarse between our lotioned fingers?
Would we feel the tiny cool bones
through the rice-paper skin of the grandmothers,
afraid we might squeeze too hard
like the pastor at the church door?
Would the limp leaf of a sick one
lie listless in our palm, distastefully?

Would the teen rush to grab the reluctant hand
of her hoped-for sweetheart?
Would the gay guys down the block
make sure to hold hands with strangers
so no one in their dangerous red state would guess?
Would those who have been hurt too often shrink from contact
or freeze in numb compliancy
and afterward tell themselves no one else was there?
Would we feel a thrum of warm electricity
as the chain, completed, worked an alchemy
in our disparate hearts
enough to help us love needing all these others
to perfect our circle?
Would some only come if they could keep
one arm free for their gun?

*

Sea-Rise

Lofoton, like those fair isles of myth
where the magical folk retreated
as humans spread through their known world:
surely here we shall find what we are seeking.
Here, where the dreams of mountains
underlie their substance, coalesce
out of mist and dawn and sea-glass.
Here where it's easy to believe
heroes sleep, slumped over their unnecessary swords
in sea-sunk caverns somewhere beyond song.
Whatever your heart has lost or might long for
and hold in its cold fist like a coin of promise
must be hidden here.
These peaks lean together, sisterly
in confabulation, eyebrowed with cloud,
their slow exhalations floating in a dove-breast sky.
If you turned your eyes away for only a moment,
you might find they had sunk under rising waters,
taking the little red houses, too, like spilled berries on their skirts
into abysses of memory, like Atlantis,
where there might be stored an old wisdom how to survive
ice, storm, fire, and cupidity.
We imagine settling together at the margins
where nothing precious would be put to waste,
where our songs, too, might travel through the water,
where our sinews might make humble fishing-line
for new generations to reach into those depths,
and the temperate silver that comes shivering into our hands
would be sufficient life-currency and no more,
in this place where we might give and be given back.

*

The Icon of Extreme Humility

Farther than the eye can see on this great grey lens,
every under-ocean ear and skin
can hear the throb and roar of our coming.
We shiver their tissues, purses of delicate air,
their jellies and fluids with what should be dread,
save for their innocence of malice—
all those marine creatures.
This is my apology for blunt and blunder
by which, perhaps, we may come to begin
an infant compassion.

Our repentance stands in the grave with such sad eyes,
looking past suffering,
but holding the chastening rod,
the mocking emblem of empire, already
forgetting yesterday's deathly sting
in our old habits of majesty.

Now comes a gold crease ringing the horizon,
some steady sun leaking in from outside
this clamshell of mauve mortality.
Such a debt. Such a relenting provision
we enjoy in every molecule of grace.
On the sea floor, I can feel my heart decomposing,
trying to rise.

~

And then the operculum of weather closes over us.
We are laid down in our quiet, will or no will,
cloud-shrouded in a parsimony of waiting.

On the International Space Station up above,
someone is looking down and glimpsing the limit
of our atmosphere, this very horizon curving

away on every side, endless to our eye,
no more than a wisp to theirs, like the first
and final breath of the infant too small to survive.

~

Divers, we're not aqualunged, but tethered
in our bell-jar, with our leaded boots,
our isinglass and brass screws.

Can't see for sediment
kicked up by our own feet
among the wooden bones of our old ships,

and hungers that drive us, brave
or foolhardy, eager and dying to get
There. Not even this truth is framed for our tongue to tell.

Belled and carapaced in our canvas integument of longing,
we stride out, as though we need no umbilicus,
as though the last breath would be enough.

*

Echolocation

I click, I whistle, I announce myself. I want to know
where you are in the contrarian seascape
through which we swim, hungering for response.
Speak to me. Speak your name. Declare your place
in the order of things, your relationship
with this liquid world of shifting depths and seasons.
We must find each other through this roar and churn,
as the clear sea rises, and transmogrifies
into a Gorgon-moil of torn sargasso,
or storm-culled kelp and the debris of the land.
Sipping breaths through the hurly-burly, we sink down
to quieter levels, to recover from
the heave of dodging flotsam and breasting those waves.
Then, under the calm lens of aquamarine,
the sinus-wave of our progress is our constant,
pausing to weave our looping lasso-snoods
of bubbles to constrict the herring schools
for our scooping. Our eager chat and squeals
of satisfaction are songs of collaborative joy.
Evolution sings through and saturates our tissues.
We have been fashioned to find one another
whether in silty estuary or cave of blue
mid-ocean. This we come to know:
you must listen to yourself, to your own voice
sounding out against resisting surfaces
to understand where you are, and to be found.
Identify yourself, moment by moment,
but always, at the same time, be listening;
saying, "I, here, acknowledge You, there; and here we are,
known, sounded, recognized, reconnected
in our malleable slipstream of a world.

*

Paradoxes

You can neither go forward without returning
nor retrace your way without covering new territory.
You can't know the nature of a place the first time you stand in it
nor the second, perhaps only the last, maybe not even then.
When you find yourself abandoned, you are carried.
You don't know your companion until you find yourself alone.

You will be walking the winter beach yet find your heart burning
its way out between your ribs. From the farthest promontory
your heart begins its journey across seas. Then, the next minute
you feel most landlocked, like a beast in a subterranean den,
a stranger to daylight. Solitary as a tide-surrounded rock,
you are married
to the core of things and to the holy, passionate unknown.

You could believe yourself deaf and blind, yet you are learning
that the unfolding of all mysteries is also your vision, song, and
      story.
When others want greatness from you, your heart slips away like
      a linnet
vanishing into the upper air, a mote, ash, dust, not even
visible to yourself. When shadowing death leaves you harried,
buried—the journey just begun opens out, and you set sail home.

*

About the Author

Jennifer M Phillips is a bi-national poet living on Cape Cod, Massachusetts within sight of the Atlantic. Writing since the age of seven, Phillips has published poetry in over a hundred journals, and authored two previous chapbooks: *Sitting Safe In the Theatre of Electricity* (iblurb.com, 2020) and *A Song of Ascents* (Orchard Street Press, 2022). A poetry collection, *Wrestling With the Angel*, was published from Wipf and Stock Publishers. Two poems were nominated for a 2024 Pushcart Prize, and others have won the Princemere Prize, the Joe Gouveia Outermost Poetry Prize 2022 and 2023, The Letter Poetry Prize 2023, and Anansi Archive Poetry Prize 2023, and been shortlisted for the *Cutthroat* Joy Harjo Poetry Prize 2024. Phillips is a gardener, priest, pastel-painter, and grower of bonsai.

Journeying across boundaries and spiritual exploring have been perennial themes in Phillips' life and work. Phillips was born in Kent, and has lived in four British counties and five U.S. states. This group of poems arose from a voyage from Iceland to Svalbard and Norway in 2023. These places—like the Gulf of Maine to which Cape Cod is neighbor—are among those most dramatically impacted by the warming of planetary climate change. It is important for poets and artists to see and bear witness to the world in its changes in ways that touch hearts and minds, and yet every journey we make must be weighed for its cost in carbon and expended resources to the planet.

www.ingramcontent.com/pod-product-compliance
Lightning Source LLC
Chambersburg PA
CBHW022102080426
42734CB00009B/1463